CLASSIC ROCK FOR TWO

Arrangements by Peter Deneff

ISBN 978-1-5400-6545-2

HAL•LEONARD®

Visit Hal Leonard Online at
www.halleonard.com

Contact Us:
Hal Leonard
7777 West Bluemound Road
Milwaukee, WI 53213
Email: info@halleonard.com

In Europe contact:
Hal Leonard Europe Limited
42 Wigmore Street
Marylebone, London, W1U 2RN
Email: info@halleonardeurope.com

In Australia contact:
Hal Leonard Australia Pty. Ltd.
4 Lentara Court
Cheltenham, Victoria, 3192 Australia
Email: info@halleonard.com.au

BANG A GONG
(Get It On)

VIOLINS

Words and Music by
MARC BOLAN

21
25
28
32
36
39

CAN'T FIGHT THIS FEELING

VIOLINS

Words and Music by
KEVIN CRONIN

Rock Ballad

21
25
29
33
37
40
rit.
rit.

CARRY ON WAYWARD SON

VIOLINS

Words and Music by
KERRY LIVGREN

21
25
29
33
37
41

COLD AS ICE

VIOLINS

Words and Music by MICK JONES
and LOU GRAMM

22
26
31
35
39
43

COME ON EILEEN

VIOLINS

Words and Music by KEVIN ROWLAND,
JAMES PATTERSON and KEVIN ADAMS

21
25
29
33
37
40

COME TOGETHER

VIOLINS

Words and Music byJOHN LENNON
and PAUL McCARTNEY

23
28
33
38
43
48

CROCODILE ROCK

VIOLINS

Words and Music by ELTON JOHN
and BERNIE TAUPIN

21
25
29
32
36
40

DOWN ON THE CORNER

VIOLINS

Words and Music by
JOHN FOGERTY

26
31
36
42
47
52

EVERY LITTLE THING SHE DOES IS MAGIC

VIOLINS

Words and Music by
STING

26
31
37
43
47
1.
51
2.

FREE FALLIN'

VIOLINS

Words and Music by TOM PETTY
and JEFF LYNNE

Medium Rock

28
33
38
44
49
54

HURTS SO GOOD

VIOLINS

Words and Music byJOHN MELLENCAMP
and GEORGE GREEN

22
26
To Coda
30
34
38
42
D.S. al Coda
CODA

THE JOKER

VIOLINS

Words and Music by STEVE MILLER,
EDDIE CURTIS and AHMET ERTEGUN

26
31
35
39
43
47
1.
2.

LIVIN' ON A PRAYER

VIOLINS

Words and Music byJON BON JOVI,
DESMOND CHILD and RICHIE SAMBORA

19
23
26
To Coda
29
32
1.
35
2.
D.S. al Coda
CODA

MAGGIE MAY

VIOLINS

Words and Music by ROD STEWART
and MARTIN QUITTENTON

21
25
29
33
38
43

MR. ROBOTO

VIOLINS

Words and Music by
DENNIS DeYOUNG

19
Play 3 times
22
25
28
31
1.
2.

MONEY FOR NOTHING

VIOLINS

Words and Music by MARK KNOPFLER
and STING

16
19
22
25
28
1.
2.

ONE MORE NIGHT

VIOLINS

Words and Music by
PHIL COLLINS

Moderate Ballad

30
36
42
48
54
60

PEACE OF MIND

VIOLINS

Words and Music by
TOM SCHOLZ

21
24
27
30
33
36

REELING IN THE YEARS

VIOLINS

Words and Music by WALTER BECKER
and DONALD FAGEN

SMOKE ON THE WATER

VIOLINS

Words and Music by RITCHIE BLACKMORE,
IAN GILLAN, ROGER GLOVER,
JON LORD and IAN PAICE

Moderate Rock

26
To Coda
31
1.
2.
36
41
45
D.S. al Coda
CODA
1.
2.

SUMMER OF ’69

VIOLINS

Words and Music by BRYAN ADAMS
and JIM VALLANCE

Moderate Rock

21
25
29
33
D.C. al Coda
CODA
36
40

UPTOWN GIRL

VIOLINS

Words and Music by
BILLY JOEL

26
32
37
42
48
53

YOU'RE THE INSPIRATION

VIOLINS

Words and Music by PETER CETERA
and DAVID FOSTER

21
25
29
33
36
39